21st CENTURY LIVES
RADIO DJs

Debbie Foy

WAYLAND

First published in 2009 by Wayland

Copyright © Wayland 2009

Wayland
338 Euston Road
London NW1 3BH

Wayland Australia
Level 17/207 Kent Street
Sydney, NSW 2000

Senior editor: Camilla Lloyd
Designer: Simon Burrough
Picture researcher: Diana Morris

Picture Acknowledgments: The author and publisher would like to thank the following for allowing their pictures to be reproduced in this publication: Cover: Dave Hogan/Getty Images; David M Bennett/Getty Images: 18, Winnie Chang/Rex Features: 14, Nick Cunard/Rex Features: 9, David Fisher/Rex Features: 4, 8, 10, Jon Furness/Wire/Getty Images: 19, Claire Greenway/Getty Images: 21, Neal Haynes/Rex Features: 15, Rune Hellestad/Corbis: 6, Dave Hogan/Getty Images: 11, 16, Insight Visual UK/Rex Features: 13, Steve Pyke/Getty Images: 12, Simon Roberts/Rex Features: 1, 7, Michael Selvadurai: 17, Times Newpapers/Rex Features: 5, Richard Young/Rex Features: 20.

British Library Cataloguing in Publication Data:
Foy, Debbie
    Radio DJs. - (21st century lives)
    1. Disc jockeys - Biography - Juvenile literature
    I. Title
    791.4'4'028'0922

ISBN: 978 0 7502 5688 9

Printed in China

Wayland is a division of Hachette Children's Books, an Hachette UK company

www.hachette.co.uk

Contents

Chris Evans
Big Mouth Strikes Again!

Multiple Sony Gold winner Chris Evans announced the nominations of the Sony Radio Awards in April 2008.

❝ I'm down but not out. I want to get back to work and whatever I decide to do, it'll be big. ❞

Chris Evans on his big comeback, 2002

Full name: Christopher Evans

Date and place of birth: 1 April 1966, Warrington, Cheshire

Background: Chris grew up on a tough council estate in Warrington. On leaving school he worked in several low-paying jobs and at the same time travelled to Manchester to work as an unpaid assistant at Piccadilly Radio.

Best known shows: *The Big Breakfast* Television show – Channel 4 Television (1992–93); *Radio 1 Breakfast Show* (1995–97); *Virgin Radio Breakfast Show* (1997–2001). Chris currently presents the *Weekday Drivetime Show*, Radio 2 (5–7pm).

Looks like: In the early days of his career Chris was known for his shock of red hair and trademark glasses that gave him a very distinctive appearance.

DJ style: Chris Evans was one of the first DJs to employ the 'team' format with several co-presenters all contributing to the show. In his early days his style of presenting was hyperactive and he would at times cheekily offend or insult his co-presenters or callers to the show.

Awards or achievements: Music Radio Personality of the Year, Sony Radio Awards 2006 and 2007; Entertainment Award, Sony Radio Awards 2007.

Something you might not know about him: In his younger days Chris revealed his entrepreneurial spirit by setting up his own kiss-o-gram and private detective agencies!

Chris moved to London in the late 1980s and landed a slot on Greater London Radio (GLR). In 1992 Evans moved to Channel 4 to launch *The Big Breakfast*. His manic charm and quirky interview technique resulted in huge audience figures and Chris Evans was catapulted into national stardom. In 1993 Chris formed his own company called Ginger Productions that produced two highly successful variety shows. *Don't Forget Your Toothbrush*, aired on Saturday nights, and *TFI Friday* for Channel 4 on Friday evenings. The public couldn't get enough of him!

In 1995 Chris was asked to present the *Radio 1 Breakfast Show*. Though his arrival boosted the audience figures, his relationship with Radio 1 bosses broke down and when Chris failed to turn up for work in 1997, he was dismissed from the station.

Months later, he began presenting the breakfast show on Virgin Radio. He was an instant hit and in 1998 Chris bought Virgin Radio from its owner, Richard Branson. But trouble seemed to follow Chris and again he lost his job when he failed to turn up for work.

Chris Evans on his first day hosting the Radio 1 Breakfast Show, *April 1995.*

Chris married pop singer Billie Piper in 2001 and disappeared from public life for a year or so, but in 2005 he made a comeback at Radio 2 where he currently presents the 5–7pm drivetime show. His arrival on the show was met with over 1,000 complaints from listeners but if the Sony Awards of 2006 and 2007 are any measure of his success, it looks as though Chris Evans will be going strong for some time to come …

Whether you love him or loathe him there is no denying that Chris Evans is a pioneer in broadcasting. In the early '90s everything Chris Evans touched turned into a great success. He ruled the airwaves with his quick-fire, sarcastic and mocking presenting style, gaining a cult status among his young listeners.

Chris didn't have an easy childhood. His father died when he was 13 and, seeing himself as the new breadwinner of the family, Chris took on several jobs including working in a local newsagent, getting up at 5am to arrange newspaper rounds. After leaving school he tried everything from busking in shopping centres to working on market stalls to earn a living. In the meantime, he was travelling from Warrington to Manchester to work as an unpaid assistant at Piccadilly Radio.

"He's back and he's brilliant. He's done his homework, knows the Radio 2 audience and targets them brilliantly. Chris Evans is on absolute top form – sharp, natural, articulate, entertaining and engaging. We salute his return to the airwaves …"

BBC Radio 2, Sony Radio Awards, www.radioawards.org, 2007

Chris Moyles
Radio 1's 'Saviour'

Although Chris's TV appearances have been limited, in 2006 he reached the semi-finals of X-Factor: Battle of the Stars!

"It is so easy to be smooth Mr DJ, with jokes where you can see the punch-line coming a mile off, but I just got bored doing that. Great radio is when people don't get out of their car because they want to hear what you are going to say next - but that does not mean I'm rude. I'm never rude for the sake of it ..."

Interview with Decca Aitkenhead, www.guardian.co.uk, 1999

Full name: Christopher David Moyles

Date and place of birth: 22 February 1974, Leeds

Background: As a teenager he worked at a hospital radio station and did a stint as the in-store DJ at Topshop in Leeds. He left school with 5 GCSEs and joined Aire FM (now Radio Aire) in Leeds, occasionally acting as a stand-in presenter.

Best known for: The Chris Moyles Show, Radio 1, weekday mornings 7–10am.

Looks like: A very ordinary guy you might meet on the street. Chris prefers the dressed down look complete with stubble and he has a 'low maintenance' approach to his image!

DJ style: His team members are Comedy Dave (Vitty), Aled Jones, Rachel Jones and Dominic Byrne. They are an integral part of his show. He is famous for his laddish, near-the-knuckle humour, his short temper and his barrage of put-downs directed at everything and everyone!

Awards or achievements: In 1998, after only nine months on Radio 1, Chris won the Silver Sony Radio Award for DJ of the Year. In 2006 he won a Gold Sony Radio Award for Best Entertainment Show. He has also written two autobiographies: The Gospel according to Moyles: The Story of One Man and his Mouth (2006) and Chris Moyles: The Difficult Second Book (2007).

Something you might not know about him: At the age of 18 Chris went to Europe to work on the world famous Radio Luxembourg. Here he presented as 'Chris Holmes' which was his mother's maiden name, rather than Chris Moyles.

Chris's DJ delivery comprises fast and furious outbursts mixed with long pauses, which add to his humour and appeal.

Chris Moyles is a brilliant radio host, a comedian, a best-selling author, and a genius – or so he says ... A larger-than-life character with a mouth that has sometimes caused people to burst into laughter and splutter over their morning cornflakes, Chris Moyles's career in radio started at an early age. As a teenager he worked at a hospital radio station followed by a stint as the in-store DJ at Topshop in Leeds. After working at a variety of local radio stations including Stoke, Bristol and Milton Keynes, Chris landed himself a job at London's Capital FM in 1996. There he presented *The Late Bit* each weekend and through his late-night antics, such as impersonating other DJs or rudely cutting off callers, he developed a loyal fan base.

His mouthy and brash-but-funny presenting style soon caught the attention of Radio 1 bosses and in 1997 he joined the station to present the early morning slot 4–7am. Moyles styled himself as the 'Saviour of Radio 1' as he appealed to new listeners and made the station popular again. At the age of 23 Chris was the second youngest DJ ever to present on Radio 1.

In his first year at the station, Chris's abrasive style offended many of his fellow DJs, including Mark and Lard, Simon Mayo and John Peel. However, on 8 May 1998, after only nine months on Radio 1, Chris won the Silver Sony Award for DJ of the Year.

Chris is known for hosting bizarre phone-in competitions and for his crazy jingles (in which he often pokes fun at himself and his team) that form part of his show.

In January 2004 Chris Moyles took over the breakfast show slot from Sara Cox. Backed by a huge publicity campaign comprising TV adverts, billboards and newspaper articles, and armed with new jingles, features and catchphrases, Chris took the breakfast time slot by the scruff of the neck and made it a phenomenal success. The highest paid DJ in radio with a devoted army of millions of listeners, it appears that Chris Moyles has proved his status as the 'saviour' of Radio 1.

"He has one of those minds that go all over the shop, which is partly what makes his chitter chatter on radio so brilliant ..."

Interview with Deborah Ross, www.independent.co.uk/news, 2007

Christian O'Connell
The Thinking Person's DJ

Christian scoops a Sony Gold Award in 2007 in the Best Competition category for Who's Calling Christian?

❝ With radio it's like I'm a kid in a sweetshop. I'd be happy to spend the rest of my existence doing radio shows – even if it was some local community station in the Australian outback ... ❞

Christian O'Connell on his love for radio, *The Observer*, 2006

Full name: Christian O'Connell

Date and place of birth: 1974, Winchester

Background: Chris wanted to be a DJ from an early age but as a teenager he was sacked from a hospital radio show and demo tapes he took along to his local radio station were ignored. On leaving school he did a degree in Media at Nottingham Trent University.

Best known for: *The Christian O'Connell Breakfast Show*, Absolute Radio (previously called Virgin Radio), weekdays 6–10am

Looks like: Quite smart and serious-looking, you can imagine him working in an office.

DJ style: Lots of clever, witty chat. Avoids 'laddishness' of other popular DJs. Loves bringing comedy to his shows with wacky features and phone-ins.

Awards or achievements: In 2004 he won a Sony Radio Academy Gold Award for DJ of the Year and a Silver Award for Breakfast Show of the Year. In 2005 he was presented with Sony Gold Awards for Entertainment and Breakfast Show of the Year. In 2006 he received a Sony Gold Award for Best Sports Programme (*Fighting Talk*) and in 2007 a Gold Award for Best Competition (*Who's Calling Christian?*).

Something you might not know about him: While at college Christian worked as a dustbin man to earn some extra money over the Christmas holidays.

Christian O'Connell is married and has two daughters. With his 4.30am starts, he doesn't have time for the 'showbiz' kind of life, nor does he like the rowdy, mouthy attitude of some of the popular DJs today. Instead, his witty, intelligent chat has attracted a wealth of awards and a loyal following of listeners who tune in each morning to be entertained …

Christian had always wanted to be a DJ but didn't get his big break until he was 25. Though he tried to break into hospital radio and did some work as a stand-up comedian, after his degree he ended up in a sales job. It was his wife Sarah who suggested he try to get into radio 'through the back door' by getting a job in sales at a radio station, and then persuading someone to take him on as a DJ.

In 2001 Christian joined the London indie music station Xfm to present *The Breakfast Show*. The listener ratings went up and over the next few years Christian won several Sony Radio Awards, including one for his Radio 5 Live Saturday morning sports show, *Fighting Talk*, that he presented alongside the Xfm breakfast slot.

In 2006 Christian joined Virgin Radio (now Absolute Radio) to present the breakfast show – his first high profile national radio show. He got off to a great start with his highly successful feature '*Who's Calling Christian?*' in which listeners are asked to persuade celebrities to ring the show in the hope of winning £10,000 to donate to a charity of their choice. The celebrities Steven Spielberg, Kiefer Sutherland, Sir Roger Moore and Tony Blair have all rung the show live on air, and due to its success Christian was presented with another Sony Radio Academy Gold Award in 2007.

Christian is dedicated to his job and spends hours trawling magazines, newspapers and websites to find ideas for his show and snippets of entertaining news that will make his banter interesting for his listeners.

Christian delivers his chat with a dry sense of humour and an ironic style.

With this kind of dedication Christian looks set to entertain you over your morning tea and toast for a long while to come.

"At school he was told off for being a chatterbox and a daydreamer, but he's managed to make a career of both. Now he has brought his brand of intelligent chat and cheek to Virgin's Breakfast Show and he can't believe his luck."

Interview with Lynn Barber, *The Observer*, 2006

Jo Whiley
Radio Rock Goddess

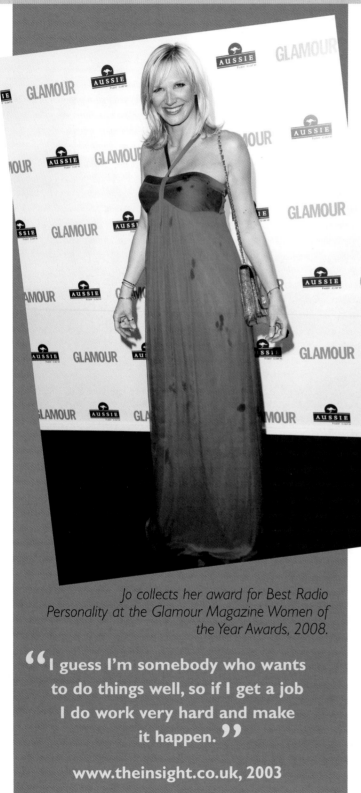

Jo collects her award for Best Radio Personality at the Glamour Magazine Women of the Year Awards, 2008.

" I guess I'm somebody who wants to do things well, so if I get a job I do work very hard and make it happen. "

www.theinsight.co.uk, 2003

Full name: Johanne Whiley

Date and place of birth: 4 July 1965, Northampton

Background: Her interest in music was forged through a very close relationship with her sister Frances, who is also a DJ and has a genetic mental disorder. Unsure of what she wanted to do when she left school Jo studied languages at Brighton Polytechnic. After a temporary job at BBC Radio Sussex in which she attended gigs and interviewed musicians, Jo attended City University in London to do a course in Radio Journalism.

Best known for: *The Jo Whiley Show*, Radio 1, weekdays 10am–12.45pm. A feature on the show *Live Lounge* invites artists into the studio to perform new material.

Looks like: Glam and fashionable, she is often pictured with her children and looks like a really cool mum!

DJ style: Self-assured, positive and upbeat.

Awards or achievements: DJ of the Year at Sony Radio Awards 1998. Jo was also voted Best Radio Personality at the Glamour Women of the Year Awards 2008.

Something you might not know about her: When she was young Jo swam competitively for her home county of Northamptonshire.

Jo is known for her ability to spot the music industry's next big thing.

Jo Whiley is one of the most credible female DJs in a mostly male world of radio. Whether she is presenting at Glastonbury Festival or broadcasting her playlists and intelligent, soft-spoken patter to millions of listeners every weekday morning, Jo Whiley seems calm and in control.

Jo's childhood taught her how to deal with crises. Her sister Frances had particular problems as a result of her disability and Jo learnt to respond to situations positively. Her close relationship with her sister and their love of music has been one of Jo's greatest inspirations.

Her first presenting job for WPFM – Radio 4's youth culture and music show – came about as a result of persistent letter writing to many radio stations. Jo then moved over into television to work as a researcher on the Channel 4 music show *The Word*, where she worked with her friend, Zoe Ball.

In 1993 Jo got her big break at Radio 1, hosting a weekday evening show called *The Evening Session* with fellow DJ Steve Lamacq. They played mainly guitar-based alternative music, broke new bands and exposed new musical trends.

From 1997 until 2001 *The Jo Whiley Show* (later called *The Lunchtime Social*) was broadcast on weekday lunchtimes. When Simon Mayo left Radio 1 in 2001,

The Jo Whiley Show moved to the mid-morning slot of 10am–12.45pm. One of the most popular features on Jo's show is the *Live Lounge* sessions in which artists, hand-picked by Jo herself, perform their new releases or cover versions of their favourite songs.

Almost every big name in music has been either a live guest on *The Jo Whiley Show* or has featured in *Live Lounge*. Over the years she has conducted in-depth interviews with some of the biggest stars in the music industry and when Madonna was a guest on the show the pair of them talked for hours.

In the course of her radio career Jo Whiley has earned the respect of musicians, fans and colleagues. She is married with four children and her equal passions for music, her family and her job are what drive her on.

"Chris Martin stopped a Coldplay gig to sing Happy Birthday to her down the phone, Bono got to his knees to tell her he adored her and Madonna spent three impromptu hours on her show … There is, in short, something about Jo that makes her very different from the mass of female DJs around her."

Louise Gannon interview, *Daily Mail*, February 2006

John Peel
The Champion of Alternative Music

John Peel was a much-loved DJ and a hero to millions of alternative music fans.

> " You get free records, you get paid for playing them on the radio, I choose all the music for my own programmes... it seems to me to be almost the perfect life, really... "

John Peel after collecting his OBE, 1998

Full name: John Robert Parker Ravenscroft

Date and place of birth: 30 August 1939, Heswall, Cheshire. John Peel died 25 October 2004

Background: At the age of 13 John was sent away to boarding school. A shy, quiet boy he preferred listening to his record collection to playing rugby. On leaving school John did three years compulsory National Service in the military.

Best known for: *The Peel Sessions*; many of today's best musicians have recorded a session for John Peel.

Looks like: A really cool granddad who would be great to go to a gig with!

DJ style: Direct, witty, honest, down-to-earth. John was softly-spoken, modest and managed to create an intimacy with his listeners that made people feel as though he were talking directly to them.

Awards or achievements: In 1998 John Peel was awarded an OBE (Order of the British Empire) for services to music. In 2002 he received the Sony Gold Award for his outstanding contribution to radio over 35 years of broadcasting. He was also awarded a host of Honorary Degrees and Doctorates from British universities.

Something you might not know about him: John Peel's love of Liverpool FC was so great that he named his children after the club! William Robert Anfield and Alexandra May Anfield (after the football ground, Anfield); Thomas James Dalglish (after the famous player named Kenny Dalglish) and Florence Shankly (after a famous Liverpool FC manager, Bill Shankly).

John Peel is pictured here with DJ Bailey who currently plays on Radio1 Xtra.

Before John Peel's death in 2004, he was one of Britain's most loved and respected DJs. His relaxed on-air style was reminiscent of a casual chat about music over the garden fence, but in fact John Peel was a very serious music fan who catapulted many of today's most popular bands into the limelight. Bands such as The White Stripes, Pulp, and Blur (among others) owe much of their success to John Peel's dedication to promoting new and exciting music.

Over the course of almost 40 broadcasting years, John Peel gave new bands the leg-up they needed and provided generations of young people with an exciting soundtrack for their lives. From hippy to house music, John Peel was the champion of alternative music.

In 1962, after doing his military service, John Peel flew to Texas, USA, and landed a job at a radio station in Dallas. Over the next three years he moved to various radio stations in the USA, including Los Angeles, where he hung out with some of the hippest '60s bands.

Returning to the UK John began work for Radio London, one of the first 'pirate' radio stations, broadcasting from a boat out at sea. Here he developed his reputation of promoting musicians that had not been heard of before.

In 1967 when the BBC launched its new music station, Radio 1, John left Radio London and joined the BBC.

Over the next few decades John Peel uncovered many new musical trends, such as punk, reggae and hip hop and brought a new diversity to the BBC. These musical styles weren't usually mainstream and John Peel is credited for getting them heard.

By 2000 John was presenting a show on Radio 4 entitled *Home Truths* featuring tales of ordinary, everyday folk and family life. He was also much in demand for voice-overs for TV documentaries and adverts. He enjoyed seeing the world and was commissioned by *The Daily Telegraph* newspaper as a travel writer. During a working holiday to Peru with his wife Sheila in October 2004 John Peel suffered a heart attack and died.

Bands, fans and supporters from all around the world paid tribute to John Peel. The alternative music scene had lost their champion and music fans had lost a hero.

"Perhaps it's possible that John can form some kind of nightmarish career out of his enthusiasm for unlistenable records and his delight in writing long and facetious essays."

R. H. J. Brooke, John Peel's housemaster at Shrewsbury School, Shropshire

Johnny Vaughan
The Loudmouth

After his high-energy breakfast show schedule, Johnny kicks back at the Capital Radio Christmas bash in 2006.

> **❝ I inherited London's number 1 breakfast show three years ago from a living legend with 17 years under his belt. To keep the show in the top spot with that kind of legacy has been a tremendous challenge, particularly given the intensity of the competition. The market's changed and so have we, I've got a great team around me and the show's going from strength to strength. ❞**
>
> *Media News,* **January 2007**

Full name: Jonathan Randall Vaughan

Dates and places of birth: 16 July 1966, Barnet, North London

Background: Johnny was educated at a private boarding school called Uppingham. Before becoming a DJ, he had lots of jobs including being a grill chef and a shop assistant.

Best known show: *Capital Breakfast Show* on Capital FM Radio.

Looks like: Johnny looks like a fairly ordinary guy and often wears football shirts or casual clothes. He shaved his head for charity in 2008.

DJ style: Johnny tells a lot of jokes! He does most of the talking and his co-presenters or members of the 'gang' set him up for many of his jokes.

Awards or achievements: Johnny Vaughan was nominated for a National Television Award for Most Popular Entertainer in 1998. He was presented with a Silver Sony Radio Award for the *Capital Breakfast Show* in 2008.

Something you might not know about him: Johnny is an avid Chelsea FC supporter and is married to Antonia who he met while working in a video store. They have two children, Tabitha and Rafferty.

Johnny's quick-fire style involves tomfoolery and putting on lots of accents, but he also has the ability to conduct intelligent and probing interviews.

Johnny Vaughan's entry into the world of showbiz was almost accidental. After a series of unspectacular jobs a friend invited him to watch a TV episode being filmed. Johnny was caught on camera, he sounded great, and the rest is history!

Johnny Vaughan began presenting Channel 4's *The Big Breakfast* in 1997. From 1997 until 2001 weather girl and actress Denise Van Outen partnered him in this morning show. Her cheeky personality and his quick wit ensured that the successful duo raised audience figures to record levels.

In 2003 Johnny began presenting *Fighting Talk*, BBC Radio 5 Live's sports debate show, but in 2004 when Chris Tarrant left the *Capital Breakfast Show* after 17 years, Johnny Vaughan stepped in. Both on- and off-air his delivery is fast and furious, often bouncing obscure facts and ideas around in quick succession. His audience has found his 'cheeky chappie' wit and charm engaging.

Johnny's radio show has featured co-presenters in addition to the 'breakfast gang' of his production team.

In January 2008 Denise joined Johnny on the *Capital Breakfast Show with Johnny Vaughan* in the hope of recreating some of their old magic and boosting the number of listeners. Denise left the show in the summer of 2008 and was replaced by the ex-model Lisa Snowden in August 2008. She hosts the television reality show *Britain's Next Top Model* and was a contestant in *Strictly Come Dancing* in 2008. She has proved to be an enthusiastic and very popular co-presenter.

"An adrenaline rush of boundless energy and enthusiasm, Johnny Vaughan gets London buzzing every morning. With a deft turn of phrase, the ability to enliven the mundane and unparalleled story-telling prowess, Johnny manages to convey a strong sense of community spirit in London. The indefatigable Johnny Vaughan has become the essential wake-up call for the capital."

Judges' comments; www.radioawards.org/winners, 2008

T039108

Nihal
At the Forefront of Asian Music

Nihal is one of the few DJs to present both mainstream and specialist music shows.

"I love doing it. I love the medium of radio. I happen to be a genuinely noisy person who is also a music junkie, so radio is perfect for me."

Interview with Arifa Akbar, *The Independent*, 14 January 2008

Full name: Nihal Arthanayake

Date and place of birth: 1 June 1971, Essex

Background: Nihal's parents came to the UK from Sri Lanka in the 1960s. Nihal first love was rap music and he began promoting rap shows while he was still at school.

Best known show: *Weekend Breakfast Show*, Radio 1, Saturday and Sunday, 7–10am

Looks like: Cheeky and boyish with a wide grin, trendy shoulder-length curly hair and beard.

DJ style: Nihal has a friendly, chatty style and likes to do lots of 'shout outs' between tracks.

Awards or achievements: Sony Gold Radio Award (2003) – Specialist Music Category for *Bobby Friction and Nihal Present.*

Something you might not know about him: Nihal has been a loyal Tottenham Hotspurs FC supporter since his father first took him to a match when he was a boy.

Nihal (far left) and Bobby Friction (far right) host a session at Radio 1 with Dhruva (second left) and Sharmaji (third left) from South Asian electronic music group, Sub Swara.

Nihal is a highly talented and popular DJ who came to broadcasting through music. Hardworking and determined, Nihal has worked in most areas of the music industry. As well as being a promoter of rap music, he has also been a recording artist. After graduating from university he was signed to a major record label and rapped with popular artists such as Fun Da Mental and Punjabi MC.

As a music journalist, Nihal wrote for magazines such as *The Face* and *MixMag*, and in the late '90s he worked in music PR (public relations) dealing with artists such as Nitin Sawhney, Judge Jules and Elton John.

Nihal joined Radio 1 in 2002 when he was asked to co-host the *Asian Beats* show with DJ Bobby Friction. In 2003 the show was presented with a Gold Sony Radio Award. The show is now called *Bobby Friction and Nihal* and broadcasts every Wednesday, 12-2am. It promotes Asian artists and their music.

From May 2007 Nihal began to host the daily mid-morning phone-in show on BBC Asian Network. He was also asked to stand-in for Chris Moyles, Edith Bowman and Colin Murray when they were away, but in October 2007 Nihal began presenting the *Weekend Breakfast Show* on Saturday and Sunday mornings. Finally Nihal had hit the big time, becoming one of the first Asian DJs to move across into mainstream radio.

Nihal has always celebrated his differences, is proud of his heritage and regularly gets emails and texts from listeners who say that it is great to have a British Asian voice on Radio 1.

As well as club DJing Nihal has played at gigs and festivals up and down the country, such as Glastonbury and Bestival. To give some idea of his dedication to promoting the music he loves, in 2005 Nihal played in Bangladesh, Dubai, Germany, India, Sri Lanka, Switzerland and Thailand. He also toured America with Bobby Friction. With his knowledge of music Nihal is regularly asked to appear on music-related TV shows, such as *The Brits* or *Never Mind The Buzzcocks*.

Nihal's first-hand knowledge of the music industry helps him to further new artists, but helping to promote Asian music in the UK and around the world is his first love …

"Though it is fair to say that Nihal is not yet a household name, he has risen inexorably to become one of the most important presenters in the Radio 1 schedule and the most high-profile British-Asian broadcaster."

Arifa Akbar, *The Independent*, 14 January 2008

17

Sara Cox
Ladette to Lady

Sara happily accepts the Radio Personality of the Year Award at the Glamour Magazine Women of the Year Awards, 2007.

> **A common misperception of me is that I'm a crazy party girl or a ladette, which I hate. I've had my moments...but in real life I'm a really chilled, unassuming sort of person.**
>
> *The Independent, 29 September 2007*

Full name: Sarah Joanne Cox

Date and place of birth: 13 December 1974, Bolton, Greater Manchester

Background: Sara grew up on a small farm in Bolton. She left school with 4 A-level passes and decided to pursue a career in modelling. While she was modelling she was scouted for television and began presenting on Channel 4.

Best known shows: *Radio 1 Breakfast Show* (2000–2003); Saturday Afternoon and Sunday Afternoon Shows, 1-4pm, (2005–current).

Looks like: Blonde and pretty with a twinkle in her eye and a mischievous smile.

DJ style: Sara's strong Northern accent and brash, cheeky manner sets her apart from many radio DJs and presenters. She is also down-to-earth and fun-loving.

Awards or achievements: Sony Radio Gold Award for Public Service (2000) for the show *Sunday Surgery*; Best Radio DJ, Smash Hits Awards (2001).

Something you might not know about her: Sara is an excellent horse rider and says if she wasn't a radio presenter she might even have been a professional show jumper!

Sara Cox may have been born on Friday the 13th but it certainly hasn't been unlucky for her! Witty, determined and down-to-earth with a positive attitude, Sara's successful career path saw her move from modelling to one of the most prestigious jobs in radio.

Sara spent the first seven years of her life living on her parents' farm. When Len and Jackie Cox split up, Sara, the youngest of five children, went to live with her mother.

As a child Sara had always felt that something special was going to happen to her, and at the age of 20, it did. Television producers at Channel 4 offered her the chance to co-present *The Girlie Show*. Her initial break into television was followed up in 1999 when she was asked to present the popular morning show *The Big Breakfast*.

It was around this time that Sara, and her friend Zoe Ball, were often photographed while out partying and earned themselves the nickname of 'ladettes'.

In September 1999 Sara's Radio 1 career began, co-presenting the Saturday lunchtime show. Sara (acting as 'Nurse Coxy') launched *The Sunday Surgery*, a programme that dealt with listeners' problems.

Her cheeky charm and warm, Northern wit proved to be popular with listeners and, when Zoe Ball left Radio 1 in 2000 to bring up her family, Sara took over to present the *Radio 1 Breakfast Show*. The number of listeners grew from seven to eight million in her first year in the job – higher than those of Chris Evans or Zoe Ball.

In January 2004 Sara swapped jobs with Chris Moyles. Moyles began his reign on the *Radio 1 Breakfast Show* and Sara began presenting on the drivetime slot, weekdays 3–5.45pm. Six months later Sara gave birth to her first child, a baby girl named Lola.
On her return to work in February 2005 she took over the afternoon show on Saturdays and Sundays 1–4pm.

Sara has big plans for the future, but for now she has a job she loves and in February 2008 she gave birth to her second child, Isaac. Though she says she would like to get back into television and try her hand at writing, radio will always be her first love ...

Sara at the Live 8 benefit concert in 2005.

"'She was great from the outset, but the thing that really hit me about her is that she is the same off air as on air. I really liked that because you come across lots of people who change when they go on air."

Matt Barbet, Radio 1 news presenter, *The Independent*, 8 October 2007

Zane Lowe

Hey, Mr DJ!

Zane Lowe scooped his fourth NME Award for Best Radio Show in 2008, leading Chris Moyles to jokingly refer to it as the 'Zane Lowe Award.'

" Like every kid who gets the music bug... I just wanted to rhyme, ever since I was about twelve that was all I wanted to do, just to write rhymes and rap them. And make a living from it. And it didn't really happen. So if I can't make a good living making music, I might as well make one talking about it. "

Zane Lowe, on his early music career, 2007

Full name: Alexander Zane Reid Lowe

Date and place of birth: 7 August 1973, New Zealand

Background: Bitten by the music bug at a young age, Zane loved to rhyme, rap and MC. In New Zealand he was in a hip hop group called Urban Disturbance. Feeling the desire to travel, he ended up in London where his big break came when he was offered presenting work on MTV.

Best known for: *The Zane Lowe Show*, Radio 1, Mondays to Thursdays 7–9pm. He plays a variety of alternative music including punk, rock, drum and bass and UK hip hop.

Looks like: Cool and moody with a trendy haircut, beard and chiselled features.

DJ style: Fast and enthusiastic, similar in style to a hip hop DJ behind his decks. Zane uses samples of music or interview clips and sometimes you can hear him singing along to the music!

Awards or achievements: *The Zane Lowe Show* has won Best Radio Show at the NME Awards every year from 2005 to his latest award in 2008! He also scooped the Gold Sony Radio Award in 2006.

Something you might not know about him: Zane broadcasts his shows standing up to project the energy and enthusiasm of a live 'club' event!

Zane Lowe is at the forefront of new and exciting music. One of the hippest alternative radio DJs around, Zane has a passion to expose new bands and new music that he believes in. *The Zane Lowe Show* has championed many new bands that have gone on to be very successful – among these are The Arctic Monkeys, Kasabian and The Kaiser Chiefs. Here's the 'Lowe-down' on one of our favourite DJs…

Zane grew up in New Zealand, where he was a member of a hip hop band, Urban Disturbance. He grew restless, decided to travel, and after a short stay in America, Zane Lowe arrived in London where he landed a job in a record shop. Zane brought with him a videotape of bands he had interviewed back in New Zealand and after some persistence he persuaded MTV to look at the video, and eventually to give him some presenting work. So, in 1997 Zane began presenting on the MTV show *Brand:New*. In 2002 he began presenting *Gonzo*, MTV's popular music show.

Before working for the BBC, Zane worked for several years at the London radio station Xfm, which focuses on alternative and indie music. His intelligent, engaging and amusing style soon caught people's attention and in June 2003, Zane moved to Radio 1 and began hosting his own show, taking over the slot from Colin Murray. His show initially aired three nights a week – Tuesdays, Wednesdays and Thursdays – from 8–10pm but in 2004 an additional Monday night slot was added and the time was altered to 7–9pm, which is where it remains today.

Zane Lowe is dedicated to showcasing new music on his radio show and is also a member of Breaks Co-op, a New Zealand band who have released two albums: *Roofers* (1997) and *The Sound Inside* (2005). Full of energy, drive and enthusiasm let's hope Zane sticks around on the airwaves to introduce us to more exciting new music!

"The whole fun of doing a radio show is ultimately it's really spontaneous and really live and you don't have to think about it too much. But I'd like to think that what we're doing is just getting behind the music. Making the most of the two hours that we have on the radio and just trying to employ a community spirit and bring everybody in on it. I think it's much better when everybody's involved."

www.bbc.co.uk/radio1/zanelowe/biography

Other Radio DJs

Annie Nightingdale

Born in 1942, Annie Nightingale is the longest serving broadcaster on Radio 1. To add to the awards and praise she has received, she was also Britain's first female DJ and the only female DJ in the world to have been awarded an MBE (Member of the British Empire) by the Queen. This was awarded to Annie in 2002 for her services to radio broadcasting.

Annie's media career began as a music journalist in Brighton. In 1970 her Radio 1 career was launched when she began presenting a Sunday evening show. In the late '70s she started presenting the show for which she is best known – *The Sunday Request Show*. In 1994 she moved to an overnight dance music show, called *The Chill Out Zone*.

Annie Nightingale can be heard on your radio on Saturday mornings between 5–7am. She is a champion of underground and new music, and is known for her love of a style of music known as breakbeat – a type of electronic music. She DJs at clubs and festivals all over the world and over the course of her long career she has travelled and hung out with some of the biggest names in rock music, including (in her early days) The Beatles, The Rolling Stones and The Who.

The BBC describe Annie as 'the closest thing we have got to Royalty' – which sums up her influential reign at Radio 1.

Colin Murray

Colin Murray was born on a Protestant council estate in Belfast in 1977. After being expelled from school at the age of 16, Colin began his career as a news reporter. In 2002 he reported on Channel 4's breakfast show *RI:SE*, co-hosting with Edith Bowman. Their boy-and-girl-next-door charm caught the eye of Radio 1 bosses and the *Colin and Edith Show* was launched in 2003, airing on Saturdays and Sundays, 10am-1pm.

In 2004 the *Colin and Edith Show* moved to the weekday lunchtime slot, taking over from Mark and Lard, and the audience figures rocketed to over 5 million. In June 2006 while Edith continued with the *Lunchtime Show*, Colin moved to a weeknights, 10pm–Midnight. For many music fans, this slot is still associated with John Peel, and many people wondered if Colin was able to fill the cult DJ's shoes. It appeared he was, for in 2007 Colin Murray scooped a gold at the Sony Radio Academy Awards for *Music Broadcaster of the Year*.

Colin is also the presenter of Radio 5 Live's *Fighting Talk*, a sports panel show that airs on Saturday mornings at 11am. Colin Murray is a talented and versatile DJ and presenter – perhaps watch out for him on your TV screen as well!

Edith Bowman

Edith Bowman is one of Britain's most successful radio DJs. A dedicated music fan and festival-goer, Edith currently presents her own slot on weekday afternoons, 1-4pm.

Edith was born in 1975 and raised in Anstruther, Scotland. Initially she wanted to be a PE teacher but following a stint at Radio Forth in Edinburgh, Edith was bitten by the presenting bug and decided to pursue a media career. In 1997 she landed the job of newsreader on MTV UK. Edith soon proved her worth as an excellent live presenter and in 2001 she began co-hosting *Hit Music Sunday* on Capital FM with Cat Deeley.

In 2002 Edith began co-presenting the Channel 4 breakfast show *RI:SE* with Colin Murray. Their on-screen chemistry worked and in 2003 they were invited to present the *Colin and Edith Show* on Radio 1. Going to work at Radio 1 was described by Edith as fulfilling 'a childhood dream'. In summer 2006 Edith was given her own show.

Edith's career has gone from strength to strength. She has presented everything from *Top of the Pops* to documentaries, and in 2005 Edith won *Celebrity Fame Academy*. She has packed a lot into her career, but it's likely that with Edith's determination and drive there's more to come!

Jamie Theakston

Jamie Theakston is a born radio and TV presenter and a polished all-rounder. Born in 1970 in East Sussex, Jamie attended private school then the University of North London where he studied business. He worked at Christies Auctioneers before going into television in 1989 as a presenter on the pop culture show *The O-Zone*. He went on to form a dynamic presenting duo with Zoe Ball on the Saturday morning children's show, *Live and Kicking*.

In 1999 he joined Radio 1 to present *The Sunday Lunch Show*, but left the station in 2002 to pursue an acting and TV career. He has appeared on the West End stage, in TV sitcoms and has presented on many high profile events such as *Comic Relief, Children in Need* and *The Brits*.

Jamie has presented numerous shows for Radio 5 Live including *Sportscall* and *Radio 5 Sport*, but in April 2005 Jamie joined Heart FM 106.2, to replace Jonathan ('Jono') Coleman. Jamie currently co-hosts the *Heart Breakfast Show*, 6–9am with Harriet Scott, who has co-hosted the breakfast show since she arrived at Heart FM in 2002.

Harriet and Jamie's on-air relationship is based on affectionate banter and gentle teasing, which has clear audience appeal since the show won

the Gold Award for the Best Music Personality Show at the New York Festivals in 2007, as well as the Silver Award for Entertainment at the Sony Radio Awards, 2007.

Jamie Theakston is a regular on your TV screen, but check him out on the radio, too.

Trevor Nelson

Trevor Nelson has been working in music for years. Born in Hackney in 1968 Trevor's first job was in a shoe shop but his love for music guided him towards the music business, where he worked for two major record labels and hosted 'warehouse parties' at the weekends.

In 1985 he joined KISS FM, when it was still a pirate radio station. In 1996 he moved to Radio 1 and launched the UK's first national R&B (Rhythm & Blues) show, called *Rhythm Nation*. Today he is one of the busiest people in radio, hosting his Radio 1 Saturday evening show, 7–9pm; a weekly soul show on Radio 2, Wednesdays 10-11pm and his *1Xtra Breakfast Show*, weekdays 8-11pm.

Aside from his radio commitments, Trevor has released five of his own compilation albums and has appeared on countless TV shows, including judging the popular show *Just the Two of Us* in 2006 and 2007. He has showcased his musical knowledge on programmes for the BBC and for Channel 4.

Trevor has also presented the Mobo Awards (Music of Black Origin) twice and the European MTV Awards. He was awarded an MBE (Master of the British Empire) in 2002 for his services to helping young people in the UK. Trevor is a respected figure in the music industry all over the world, and looks as if he'll continue doing what he is good at for many more years to come.

Index

21st Century Lives

Contents of more books in the series:

British Olympians
978 0 7502 5946 0
Rebecca Romero
Ben Ainslie
Rebecca Adlington
Lee Pearson
Sarah Storey
Chris Hoy
Eleanor Simmonds
Tim Brabants
Christine Ohuruogu
Other British Olympians

Reality TV Stars
978 0 7502 5690 2
Jordan
Leona Lewis
Ben Fogle
Cheryl Cole
Kelly Osbourne
Will Young
Myleene Klass
Lee Mead
Kerry Katona
Other Reality TV Stars

Teen Movie Stars
978 0 7502 5691 9
Zac Efron
Lindsay Lohan
Daniel Radcliffe & Emma Watson
Scarlet Johansson
Hilary Duff
Freddie Highmore
Christina Ricci
Thomas Sangster
Kirsten Dunst
Other Teen Movie Stars

Radio DJs
978 0 7502 5688 9
Chris Evans
Chris Moyles
Christian O'Connell
Jo Whiley
John Peel
Johnny Vaughan
Nihal
Sara Cox
Zane Lowe
Other Radio DJs

Soap Stars
978 0 7502 5689 6
Ada Nicodemou
Jack P. Shepherd
Kara Tointon
Kym Valentine
Lacey Turner
Roxanne Pallett
Patsy Palmer
Scott Maslen
Samia Smith
Other Soap Stars

WAYLAND